Synchronicity

Synchronicity

Ben Rasnic

Kelsay Books

ISBN 13: 978-0692230022

Cover art: Joseph W. Rasnic

Kelsay Books
Aldrich Press
24600 Mountain Avenue 35
Hemet, California 92544

Acknowledgments

"Demarcations" originally appeared in *Bone Orchard Poetry*.

"The Trophy Wife" first appeared in *Brevity Poetry Review*.

"The 9 ½%," "Roots," "March Madness," "Not Your Father's NFL" and "Larimer after Dark" originally appeared in *The Camel Saloon*.

"Laundry" originally appeared in *The Clinch Mountain Review*.

"Black Dog" first appeared in *Eskimo Pie*.

"Bully" and "Thoughts on Growing Old" originally appeared in *Eunoia Review*.

"The Testosterone Equation" and "The World According to Charles Atlas" first appeared in *Gutter Eloquence*.

"Pillow Talk" originally appeared in *Ilya's Honey*.

"Monster" originally appeared in *Indigo Rising*.

"The Red Tape Flypaper Death Strip" originally appeared in *Jimson Weed*.

"Prayer" first appeared in *Kind of a Hurricane Press* "Poised in Flight" anthology.

"Skeleton Key," "Nighthawks" and "Indian Woman Passing By" first appeared in *Leaves of Ink*.

"The Awakening" originally appeared in *The Mind(less) Muse*.

"Synchronicity" first appeared in *The Orange Room Review*.

"Grilling Baby Backs" originally appeared in *Pigeon Bike*.

"The Facebook Criterion" first appeared in *Red Poppy Review*.

"The Latest Edition" originally appeared in *The Rusty Truck*.

"Cold Razor" and "Childhood Photo" first appeared in *Thirteen Myna Birds*.

Contents

The Latest Edition

arrives
before dawn,
is already old news
before it even hits
the fresh black print
of our driveway;

comes in handy
to swat the puppy
whenever he pees
on the new carpet.

The Awakening

Glistening in the essence
of Morning Star light,
it clings to the stellar fescue tips
like fresh teardrops
to a field of flashing knives;
silver linings to a world
which chooses to cloak
its thin skin
in bullet proof vests.

The Testosterone Equation

Cast into a cryptic maze
of uncertain future,

an overweight rat with blinders
ambles aimlessly
down closed corridors.

I drag myself
through the long slow winter days,
feeling woefully out of my element.

It seems
there are so few crumbs
for so many.

The heart races,
pounds the chest like
jackhammers vibrating from the stone grip
of young men in hard hats

yet even this cannot stir
the atrophied quicksand that languishes
within the soul of this paraplegic angel.

And now trapped
between indeterminate destinations
without a GPS or compass to guide me,

I long for that unforeseen enigma
to save me from floundering
& wasting my life away;

chance for me to exclaim,
"Mrs. Robinson,
I think you are trying
to seduce me."

The Trophy Wife

The trophy wife
ballooned up to twice her size
within 5 years of marriage.

To cope, her regretful husband
spent his lonely evenings
glassy-eyed in local bars.

His favorite drink
was Bloody Mary.

Meanwhile, she would sit
alone at home
watching soap operas, constantly
contemplating new designs & blueprints

to get rid of his sorry ass,
to pocket all of his money
and change her name to Sophia.

Roots

The place I call home
is no longer;
is merely a place where strangers dwell
and the memories that swelled
within those familiar walls
now belie a distant fading,
a forlorn puff of smoke waning
that escapes me now
and leaves me
with inexplicable sadness,
completely
and forever
groundless.

The 9 ½ %

9 ½ % of Americans suffer from depressive disorders
—United States Center for Disease Control.

I turn my back
against the pre-
dawn light creeping
thru shrouded drapes

finding solace
solely in deep,
blissful,
             uninterrupted sleep.

Every day
is a never-ending
monotonous cycle
             of non-events.

             Take one capsule
             daily, wait seven years
             for the FDA to acknowledge
             adverse effects.

             Outside,
             green mold slime engraves
             the vinyl siding
             like a tombstone.

Stalemate

In Junior High School,
I loved her from afar,
spent entire evenings
scripting for chance conversations.

Yet every opportunity
that availed itself
was never the right moment,

hand poised
like flypaper
over a chess board.

Laundry

When I was young,
a wise old southern gentleman
once told me,
"You can learn a lot about life
just from doing the laundry."

"First, you gotta separate the whites
from the coloreds,
else you'll find yourself
in all kinds of hot water.

The whites will lose
their shine and start to fade.
The darks will turn kinda fuzzy & gray
and if you mix the reds in there,
they'll bleed all over everything.

Leave them in the wash all together
for too long and each one'll
take on the color
of all the others

and before you know it,

you'll be damn near color blind!"

Urban Still Life

A 23-year-old female was shot in the head tonight outside of a flower and card shop. She died a short time later.

Splashes of rain
tattoo neon pools
of pitted concrete.

Pulse of random gunfire
startles the quiet,
flashes revolving sirens

in wreathes
of splattered crimson
and shattered glass.

The 10 o'clock News
punctuates the day's
events—violent and pointless;

irreconcilable episodes
between unbearable
silences.

Pillow Talk

As you lie in bed,
lay your head gently down
and dream
of black & white feathers exploding
against a background
of clear blue sky
from shotgun pepper spray;

gathered and stuffed
into factory sewn cloth
by slave wage employees
from some third world nation
to deliver
the finest plush down pillow
that money can buy

that you
may sleep well
tonight.

The World According to Charles Atlas

Mac was an easy target
for mean spirited insults &
ugly insinuations regarding
the most private inclinations
of his personal being;

was always the last one picked
for sports teams during recess
or in gym class,
always the first one out,
a strawberry insignia indelibly
tattooed onto his rib cage

or chest cavity
from the reverberating blast
of air-filled red rubber dodgeball,
typically accompanied by
uncontrolled shrieks
of wild animalistic laughter.

Had fate cast him a comic book caricature,
he would be the skinny guy on the beach
having sand kicked in his face
by the muscle bound bully
who patrolled the area
with the brunette chick hanging like a medallion
from his bulbous biceps;

a ripe candidate
to be bombarded
by commercial ads encouraging him

to bulk up his miniscule physique
and overcome his perceived enemy
by physically kicking his ass

all over the sandy beach
from here to eternity
thus winning over
the obviously shallow
& intellectually inferior female bombshell
of a prize.

I always pitied
the fool.

Nighthawks

In the strange subdued light
of silhouettes eclipsing
the evening star,

nighthawks scrape the unsettled air,
screeching across
the summer night sky

with the shriek
of nails
across a classroom chalkboard,

vanish
as suddenly
as dust.

Childhood Photo

In this black & white photo,
I am smiling, no, I am slightly grinning;
the elliptic curve of my mouth
skewed to the upper left, perhaps
from the daily routine
of butchering Elvis impersonations,
but I think more likely
from the reality
I was always ordered
to smile
whenever the camera
aimed in my direction,
yet I could never
in all honesty, totally
oblige.

Synchronicity

Grounded by a patchwork collage
of needles and clear plastic tubing,
cumbersome cables wired to snap-on electrodes
graphing signs of life--fluctuating heart rhythms,
shallow breath
choreographed by synthesized beeps & blips.

Before the turn
of the century
you held vigil by hospital bedside,
recording your father's
initial blunt force encounter
with mortality.

And now the graveyard shift nurse's starched
profile hovers at synchronized intervals
each time you emerge
from the haze of torn sleep
while in a quaint Pennsylvania borough
a groundhog sees his shadow.

Prayer

My sights have been lifted
toward a stellar cathedral
in a world without end,
an open door to the soul
of one who searches.

I pluck the soft daggers
from a millennium sky
to shear myself open,
peel away this ashen gray nest
of wounded flesh

& dissolve
within the funnel eye
of absolute light and energy;

surrender my allegiance
to empirical knowledge, my tired
arrogance cloaked in velvet robes
of quiet despair,

to take the blind leap
out of my decaying mortal element
with hands clasped, forming
silver wings

to enter the enigmatic realm
and the light of living waters.

Naked before the arc
of the flaming altar,
I am bathed in the presence
of a steady radiance, touch

of wet silk;
immerse into the echo
of infinite wisdom,

the sound of my own voice.

Cholesterol

It is rapidly
becoming a burden
to move
from one side of the room
to another,
from one room
to another, odds & ends
choking the passageways.

Life clutters
its useless junk
like cholesterol clusters
when one refuses
to relinquish
ownership.

The Facebook Criterion

I couldn't wait
to post it,
being technically, I felt,
one of the best poems
I had ever published--

concise, vibrant imagery
emanating from stone fisted verbs
seamlessly orchestrating movements
of rhythm & sound
with polished gunmetal clarity;

carefully crafted passages
neatly aligned
as pieces on a chessboard,
strategically marching toward
the final stanza's ultimate ironic twist--

only to watch it
languish, scrolling lower
and lower on the newsfeed page,

0 comments
and an Alice Johnson likes this.

Demarcations

The groundhog
population
& I
are trapped in a battle
of wills.

Lines have been crossed.

A mere layered roll
of chicken wire
buffers my vegetable garden
from the fruits
of their desire.

A 22 caliber
between the eyes
would eliminate the stand-off
& rid me
of the bane of my existence.

I tossed the gun
in the trash.

The Red Tape Flypaper Death Strip

The online application
for my dream job
required proof of citizenship

& having no green card
or INS case file number
having never resided beyond

the borders
of these United States
of America,

a birth certificate
was mandated, a piece
of paper to provide proof

that I am
who I am
and have always been,

a piece of paper
I misplaced at some point
during my 58 years

and thus
was disqualified,
the online application aborted.

Today, my wife
received in the mail
a lump sum death benefit of $255.

March Madness

The pure unadulterated sound
of composite orange ball
ricocheting from hard polished floors
captures the crowd mesmerized, anticipating
choreographed moves
like chess pieces
across the checkered squares
as in the waning seconds,
the deft artistry of
a point guard's palms spin
a perfectly inflated orb
into delicate trajectory
designed to drop gently swishing
through stringed net
ignites an explosive primal scream
of deafening proportions,
the sweet sound
of victory
at the precise second
the time clock
strikes
triple zeros.

Thoughts on Growing Old

Inevitably,
time ravages everything;
hair thins, thoughts dangle
in mid—
eyes fade, face droops,
muscles decline
& atrophy, stomachs swell,
breasts sag.

It's all too gradual
and therein lies the pain.

Would rather be doused
by a quick bucket
of cold water;
instantly melt
into a bubbling puddle of
green goo,
left smoking.

Bully

Some of the older kids carried pocket knives,
cruised the neighborhood posturing for a fight;
intimidated the physically inferior kids
& tortured small animals for kicks.

One would flash me the peace sign
then ram the fingertips between my ribs
leaving me lying helpless, gasping
for air;

used to call me "sissy" and "faggot"
for not sticking frogs
or blasting birds out of the sky
with a 40 ought shotgun;

broke my nose once for not taking a turn
at pounding the last harried breath
from the old spinster lady's beloved housecat
with the blunt end of a Louisville Slugger.

As fate would have it,
a jury of his peers sentenced him
to ten years of his adult life in federal prison
for money laundering & embezzlement…………….

Every Saturday I would walk for miles
to his parent's house on the hill
and manicure every square inch
of that immense lush green lawn
with my Murray 19-inch push mower

before the days of self-propelled
back when $10 for only 4 hours hard labor
was an opportunity I couldn't pass up

even when it meant
missing Little League practice;
even when the Yankees were playing
on the black & white at home;

even when it meant
having ice cold water poured down my back
every time I went to the back door
to collect my pay.

And I would hear his shrill laughter
echoing in my ears like
the sharp cry of a distressed cat
or the little girl scream of a defenseless victim
lying helpless before the testosterone rage
of misguided young men.

Larimer after Dark

(Denver, 1986)

Skyscrapers poise
ornamented gargoyles
guarding the complex Infra-
structure of downtown
Denver, buffer zone
fortressing

Corporate America
from the jagged edge
of inner city apocalypse.

Symphony of headlights
crescendos in pools
of black asphalt illuminating
Seventeenth Street
nightlife hopping
with bars and coffeehouses vibrant
with poetry and jazz humming
to the beat of the streets;

al fresco restaurants
on Larimer Square
catering upwardly mobile
young urban entrepreneurs
spinning wheels of fortune and rolling the dice
on blue chip stocks while chatting of
liquid assets and venture capital;

drinking margaritas
from petite marble tabletops;
Wall Street cowboys
shooting from the hip
on real estate developments
south of Littleton;

oblivious to the underbelly a few blocks north
where the buzz of neon fades
to burned out fluorescents
along gray fringe of vacant skid row

warehouses, havens
for transients, lost souls and winos
sucking blood from a bottle,
pawn shops and
pool rooms and a sign that reads
"No Children After Five O'clock"

seedy corner bars intersected
with switchblades,
Saturday Night Specials

revolving flashing lights
of ambulatory morgues;
shattered Budweiser bottles,
tossed cartons from a Mexican taqueria;
picante sauce undistinguished
from dried blood;

where last call for alcohol
empties the Longhorn Saloon—patrons
pissing in the alleyways and one
drunken Indian loudly reclaiming
the Platte River for his tribe
back in Montana.

And barely visible in the smoke
and fog and haze one can almost
discern the ghosts of Bat Masterson
& Neal Cassady staggering gingerly
arm in arm toward distant railroad tracks
while others meander toward what

destiny of metal dumpsters
& cardboard shelters, oblivious
to the bellowing trumpets
of street prophets, dull
ache of cold night's
purgatory

placing a flirtatious
gamble

with the sunrise.

Skeleton Key

There comes a time
without fail
when passions subside
and stagnate.

Self-preservation
as a rule
grows a protective layer
of skin across the heart
that callouses over time.

Yet a simple notion,
a well-placed sentiment
can re-open what was
& what should always be.

The opposite of love
is indifference.

Not Your Father's NFL

Gliding with the liquid grace
of the eagle's wings boldly engraved
into the sides of his reflective
metallic headgear;

with outstretched gloved hands
soaring toward the deepest
corner of end zone, his
taut, sinewy tissues almost burst

from the effort to snare
the oblong pigskin--first securing
a precarious fingertip grip then quickly
cradling to the chest

before landing in a fetal position at the feet
of the man with the black & white
striped shirt frantically thrusting both arms
into air to signal touchdown!

and 6 points for the home team
to which the player responds
by spiking the prize point blank into turf
then breaking into spastic gyrations

that, if just tuning in.
one could only interpret
as some form of ritualistic
ceremonial victory dance

contradicting the curiously subdued
response of the home crowd
& the subtle sarcasm
of color commentators

as the Jumbo-tron scoreboard
juxtaposes the sad-eyed disillusionment
of a freckle faced eight year-old

clad in midnight green
and a final score reading
Redskins twenty-seven, Eagles fourteen.

Cold Razor

Blood in the snow………………..

Shards of soft white moonlight
slice through a lather
of dark trees.

Cloaked in the long shadows,
the unmistakable tracks
of an assassin

align cat-like
along the edge
of the woods—

the snap of low branches
beneath a flutter of wings;

shriek of white silence.

Monster

Because he is different,
he is assumed evil and forced to hide
within the confines of a cold, dark castle
high above in the cliffs.

The villagers huddle below,
brave in numbers, becoming a singular
mindset motivated by simple catch phrases
and a stubborn aversion
to the Socratic method.

With angry diatribes,
kerosene lit torches and the guns
they love so dearly held high
amid the swirling orange flames,
they go in search of the monster,

blind to its mirror image
vacillating in the full moon
glassy-eyed reflections
of their compatriots.

Black Dog

Black dog
shivers at my door,
flicking silvery beads
from a puppet wire
baptismal rain;

coils itself
into a cheap dollar store
welcome mat;
rolled-up yellowing newspaper
marking its turf.

G.I. JOE

You bring out the worst in me.

Your plastic façade & carrousel lies
have awakened this toy soldier
that has finally assembled
the will to survive.

Humming to the tin cadence
of alkaline drum rolls,
the killer I never knew existed
is now ever ready, prepared

to defend —wind me up
and I will
rat-a-tat-tat
your brains into oblivion;

so you'd better be careful
what bridges you burn; better
build your blocks
slowly…………………………..

Grilling Baby Backs

You wouldn't eat that
if you knew what went into it
she said
between bites of her veggie burger,
turkey nuggets
and tofu salad.

Yes I would
I said,
dabbing the remaining smoky bits
of barbeque sauce
from my salt and pepper beard;

Yes,
I would.

Indian Woman Passing By

Pure elegance
just waltzed
past my bay window

in a pale green sarong
swaying gently
in summer evening breeze

slowly sweeping
the soft sweet magical scent
of mango in air,

lotus petals drift,
then silently vanish
before I chance
to savor.

Twilight

Lazy afternoon
leans toward horizon;
fragrance of lilacs, rhododendron,
fresh cut of minty, green grass;

lounging in easy chairs,
we absorb our surroundings.
Sun in your hair, pearl skin
freckled and slightly bronzed;

Meadowlarks wing
through our private arboretum;
whistle a lilting melody
in the fading light.

Listening to the warm
evening, murmur of locusts;
wind whispering
through pines.

Here we are content.
Our minds centered;
our hearts at peace.
We grow old together.

About the Author

Ben Rasnic is a native of Jonesville, a small rural town in Southwest Virginia with a population <1000. His poetry has been widely published in web-based poetry venues and print journals. A Pushcart Prize nominee in 2011, Rasnic still considers as his greatest literary achievement, electing to publish two short poems by Yusef Komunyakaa while serving as editor of his college literary magazine, *Jimson Weed*, in 1978–16 years before Komunyakaa received the Pulitzer Prize for Poetry. This is Rasnic's third published volume of poetry, preceded by *Artifacts and Legends* (2012) and *Puppet* (2013). Ben currently resides in Bowie, Maryland.

Made in United States
North Haven, CT
16 October 2023

42837661R00028